PLAY 22 SCANDINAVIAN TUNES
ARRANGED FOR TWO CELLOS

FIN JENTE

JEG SER DEG SØTE LAM

GJENDINES BÅDNLÅT

VILLEMANN OG MAGNHILD

FEDER MIKKEL

FEM FÅR, FIRE GEDER

BAGLÆNS KONTRASEJRE

RAMUND HIN UNGE

SPARVENS POLSKA

SUNTA LUVA

I RIDEN SÅ

HERR MANNELIG

SCHOTTIS EFTER LURINGEN OCH SPEL-BENGTEN

NUKU, NUKU, NURMILINTU

HIMLENS POLSKA

KALLIOLLE KUKKULALLE

JOS MUN TUTTUNI TULISI

SOFA URTUBÖRN

Ó MIN FLASKAN FRÍÐA

THE HUNGRY INNOCENT / MAGÁLL HVARF ÚR ELDHÚSI

ÓLAFUR LILJURÓS

PINDSVINE REINLANDER

TRADITIONAL SCANDINAVIAN TUNES

FOR TWO CELLOS

TRANSCRIBED, ARRANGED, & COMPILED

BY KIMY PEDERSEN

COPYRIGHT ©2020 KIMY PEDERSEN

All rights reserved. No part of this publication may be reproduced, stored, distributed, or transmitted in any form or by any means, including photocopying, recording, scanning, electronic, mechanical methods, or otherwise, except as permitted under Section 107 or 108 of the 1976 United States Copyright Act, without the prior written permission of the author, in the case of brief quotations embodied in reviews and certain other noncommercial uses permitted by copyright law. Requests to the author and publisher for permission should be addressed to the following email: kimypedersen@gmail.com.

Layout design & illustrations by Lindsey Blakely.

Table of Contents

INTRODUCTION 1

NORWAY

Fin Jente 2
Jeg Ser Deg Søte Lam 3
Gjendines Bådnlåt 4
Villemann og Magnhild 5

DENMARK

Feder Mikkel 6
Fem Får, Fire Geder 7
Baglæns Kontrasejre 8
Ramund Hin Unge 10

SWEDEN

Sparvens Polska 12
Sunta Luva 13
I Riden Så 14
Herr Mannelig 15
Schottis efter Luringen och Spel-Bengten 18

FINLAND

Nuku, Nuku, Nurmilintu 19
Himlens Polska 20
Kalliolle Kukkulalle 22
Jos mun Tuttuni Tulisi 24

ICELAND

Sofa Urtubörn 25
Ó Min Flaskan Fríða 26
The Hungry Innocent / Magáll Hvarf úr Eldhúsi 27
Ólafur Liljurós 29

NORWAY/DENMARK

Pindsvine Reinlander 30

FIN JENTE
JEG SER DEG SØTE LAM
GJENDINES BÅDNLÅT
VILLEMANN OG MAGNHILD
FEDER MIKKEL
FEM FÅR, FIRE GEDER
BAGLÆNS KONTRASEJRE
RAMUND HIN UNGE
SPARVENS POLSKA
SUNTA LUVA
I RIDEN SÅ
HERR MANNELIG
SCHOTTIS EFTER LURINGEN OCH SPEL-BENGTEN
NUKU, NUKU, NURMILINTU
HIMLENS POLSKA
KALLIOLLE KUKKULALLE
JOS MUN TUTTUNI TULISI
SOFA URTUBÖRN
Ó MIN FLASKAN FRÍÐA
THE HUNGRY INNOCENT / MAGÁLL HVARF ÚR ELDHÚSI
ÓLAFUR LILJURÓS
PINDSVINE REINLANDER

Introduction

I have been interested in traditional folk music for many years. The fact that it has been passed down for generations, and sometimes centuries, fascinates me. Traditional folk music conveys the stories, values, and history of a culture. It enriches our lives in numerous ways, from accompanying dances and soothing restless children to expressing feelings and emotions.

For the last five years, I've studied Celtic (Irish, Scottish, English) music every summer at the Santa Cruz Community Music School's Teen Camp. With each passing year that I've been playing the cello at this summer program, I've become more and more impressed with not only the beauty of the music, but also the way traditional Celtic music has been preserved and kept alive. I then started looking into other kinds of traditional music, and became drawn to traditional Scandinavian folk music, particularly because of my personal connection to it through my Norwegian and Danish family lineage. As I discovered more about this music, I found that it was not as widely documented as some other forms of folk music. I made it a mission to find and transcribe Scandinavian folk music and keep it in an accessible form to hopefully increase its visibility and performance. When transcribed onto sheet music, it becomes a historical document to preserve the culture and history for future generations.

I chose to arrange the music I found for two cellos in order to give more melodic presence to the cello, an instrument that is often assigned to an accompaniment role. As a cellist, I had a personal motivation to do this. Many of these songs are easy for cellists of all levels to play. I hope this songbook brings joy to many musicians, and keeps traditions alive.

I want to thank my cello teacher, Renata Bratt, for guiding me and helping me learn how to transcribe and set melodies, and compose accompaniments. I also want to thank my music teacher and choir director, Alex Koppel, for guiding me through the intricacies of using notation software and helping me structure this project as an independent study. They both open-heartedly supported and believed in me and my project, and I will always remember their enthusiasm and kindness.

Kimy Pedersen

Fin Jente

Pretty Girl

Trad. Norwegian waltz
Arr. Kimy Pedersen

Jeg Ser Deg Søte Lam
I See You, Sweet Lamb

Trad. Norwegian waltz
Arr. Kimy Pedersen

Gjendines Bådnlåt
Gjendine's Lullaby

Edvard Grieg
From Kaia Gjendine Slålien
Trad. Norwegian lullaby
Arr. Kimy Pedersen

This lullaby comes from Kaia Gjendine Slålien (1871-1972), a Norwegian woman who lived in the Jotunheimen mountains. She met Norwegian composer Edvard Grieg (1843-1907) at Skogadalsbøen (a cabin owned by the Norwegian Trekking Association) while she was working there as a milkmaid. Gjendine would sing for Grieg and he transcribed many of her folk songs. Her music also inspired several of his own compositions.

LYRICS

Barnet legges i vuggen ned
Stundom gråter og stundom ler (x2)
Sove nå, sove nå, i Jesu navn
Jesus bevare barnet (x2)

Mamma tar meg på sitt fang
danse med meg att og fram (x2)
Danse så, med de små
Danse så, så skal barnet sleep (x2)

The child is laid in the cradle
Sometimes crying, sometimes laughing
Sleep now, sleep now, in Jesus' name
Jesus, protect this child

Mother takes me in her lap
Dances with me to and fro
Dance like so, with the small ones
Dance like so, so the children will sleep

Villemann og Magnhild

The Wild Man and Magnhild

Trad. Norwegian
Arr. Kimy Pedersen

This Norwegian ballad is from medieval times, and these are the known verses. There are likely more. Villemann og Magnhild tells the story of Villemann "The Wild Man" rescuing Magnhild, a woman who has been caught by a troll. He plays his golden harp and distracts the troll so Magnhild can escape.

Then, the troll gets upset and unleashes his wrath, but the Wild Man is also able to take the troll's strength away and obtain it as his own.

The fairest linden leaf represents Magnhild, as the linden tree is a symbol for love and beauty. There also seem to be magical runes that want the Wild Man's rescue mission to succeed, and may be influencing its outcome.

LYRICS

Villemann gjekk seg te storan å
- Hei fagraste lindelauvi alle -
Der han ville gullharpa slå
- For de runerne de lyster han å vinne -

Villemann gjenge for straumen å stå
Mesterleg kunne han gullharpa slå

Han leika med lente, han leika med list
Og fugelen tagna på grønande kvist

Han leika med lente, han leika med gny
Han leika Magnhild av nykkens arm

Men då steig trolli upp or djupaste sjø
Det gjalla i berg og det runga i sky

Då slo han si harpe til bonns i sin harm
Og utvinner krafti av trollenes arm

The Wild Man went down to the river
- to the fairest of all the linden leaves -
Where he wanted to strike the golden harp
- For the runes wanted him to win -

The Wild Man went to stand at the stream
Masterfully he could strike the golden harp

He played it with care, he played it cunningly
The birds were calmed in the green trees

He played it softly, he played it loudly
He played Magnhild out from the troll's arms

But then the troll rose up from the depths of the sea
It rumbled in the mountains and thundered in the sky

But he struck the harp with all of his fury
And obtained the strength from the troll's arms

Feder Mikkel
Dance from Himmerland, Denmark

Trad. Danish
Arr. Kimy Pedersen

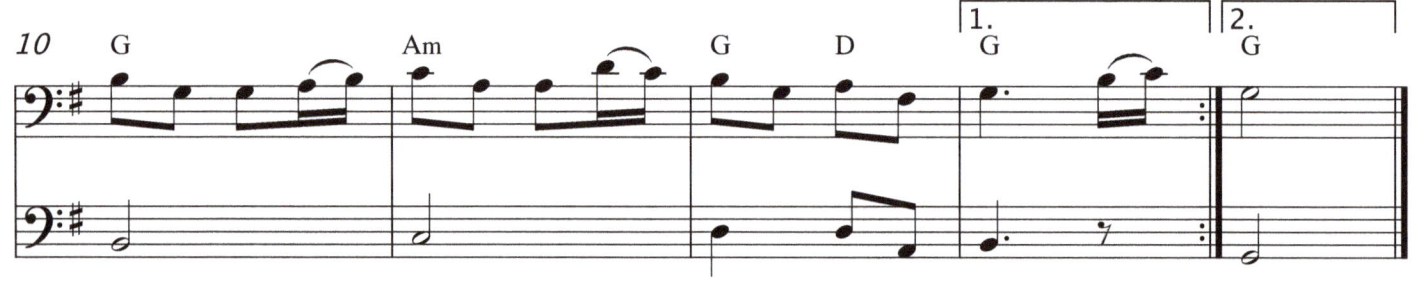

Feder Mikkel is a Danish set dance from Himmerland. In this dance, six couples will form in two lines and perform a chassé, pivot, polka, sidestep, and walk six times, one time for every couple. The dance is accompanied by this tune!

Fem Får, Fire Geder

Five Sheep, Four Goats

Trad. Danish
Arr. Kimy Pedersen

Baglæns Kontrasejre
Backwards Kontrasejre

Trad. Danish
Arr. Kimy Pedersen

The baglæns kontrasejre (backwards contra dance) is a Danish folk dance where four couples will form a square and rotate counterclockwise, with one inside arm joining the others at shoulder height. A kontrasejre (contra dance) will usually be accompanied by a certain song. In this case, the baglæns kontrasejre is accompanied by this tune!

Ramund Hin Unge

Ramund the Young

Trad. Danish
Arr. Kimy Pedersen

Ramund Hin Unge is a medieval Danish ballad about a young man named Ramund who is sent to slay seven trolls and then mercilessly kills other various creatures and takes their gold and jewels. He then sails to the Emperor's estate and horrifies everyone with his bad manners. Ramund challenges the Emperor to a duel. Although the Emperor begs him not to, and bribes him with half his kingdom and marriage to his daughter, Ramund kills him and takes the kingdom anyway.

There are around 25 known verses of this ballad, and these are just some of the verses.

LYRICS

Ramund var sig en bedre mand
om han havde bedre klæder
Dronningen gav hannem klæder på stand
af blågarn, bast og læder
"Sådant vil jeg ikke ha," sagde Ramund.
"Sådant står mig ikke bra," sagde Ramund hin unge

"Bast og blårgarn er værre end ry,
det kan du gi' tjenerne dine."
Frøkenen gav hannem klæderne ny
af silke og sammet fine
"Sådant vil jeg heller' ha'," sagde Ramund.
"Sådant står mig meget bra," sagde Ramund hin unge.

Ramund gik sig ved salten søstrand
der så han syv jætter stande
"Tager jeg Ramund på min mindste hånd
og kaster ham langt fra lande"
"Det gør ikke ene du," sagde Ramund
"I må komme alle syv," sagde Ramund hin unge

Ramund tog til sit dyre sværd
det han kaldte dymlingen røde
Hug han de jætter syv med en færd
at blodet randt dennem til døde
"Der ligger alle syv," sagde Ramund
"Alt står jeg her endnu," sagde Ramund hin unge

Kejseren ud af vinduet så
med angst og sorrigfuld mine
"Hvo er den mand, i gården mon stå
og der så hæsselig grine?
"Det er mig, jeg har lyst," sagde Ramund
"Med dig at vov' en dyst," sagde Ramund hin unge

Ramund tog til sin store kniv
den han kaldte dymlingen dyre
Skilte han kejseren ved hans liv
at hovedet fløj femten mile
"Jeg mente den ej bed," sagde Ramund
"Dog rinder blodet ned," sagde Ramund hin unge

Ramund would be a better man,
if he had better clothes
the Queen gave him clothes
made of blue yarn, bast and leather
"I don't want these," said Ramund
"I don't like these," said Ramund the Young

"Bast and blue yarn are bad for my reputation,
you can give these to your servants."
The lady gave him new clothes
of fine silk and velvet
"I'd rather have these," said Ramund
"This looks very good to me," said Ramund the Young

Ramund walked by the salty sea,
he saw seven giants standing there
"I'll take Ramund with my smallest hand,
and cast him out a long way from the land."
"You can't do that alone," said Ramund
"All seven of you must come," said Ramund the Young

Ramund drew his dear sword,
he called it The Red Dowel.
He hit all seven giants with a single slash,
and they all bled to death
"Here lies all seven," said Ramund
"And I still stand here," said Ramund the Young

The Emperor looked outside his window
with anxiety and sorrow
"Who is that man standing in the yard,
who laughs so hideously?"
"It is me, I want," said Ramund
"To fight a duel with you," said Ramund the Young

Ramund drew his big knife,
he called it The Precious Dowel.
He parted the Emperor from his life
the head flew fifteen miles.
"I didn't mean any harm," said Ramund.
"However the blood flows down," said Ramund the Young.

Sparvens Polska

Sparrow's Polska

Trad. Swedish polska
Arr. Kimy Pedersen

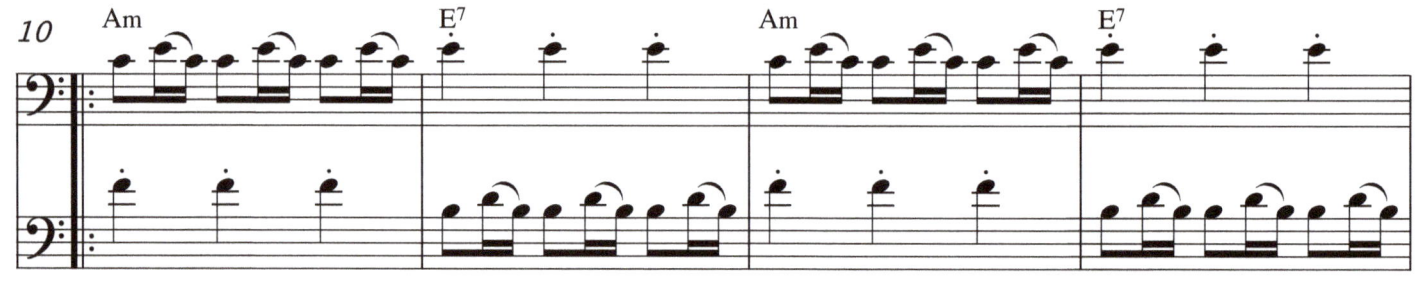

LYRICS

Å Silibrand körde uppå höga loftessvala
Allt under den linden så gröna
Där fick han se sin dotter i lunden fara
I riden så varliga genom lunden med henne

Å välest mig välest mig vad jag nu ser
Allt under den linden så gröna
Jag ser min dotter hon kommer till mig
I riden så varliga genom lunden med henne

Å Silibrand fämnar ut kap-pan så blå
Allt under den linden så gröna
Där föder hon två karska svenbarnen på
I riden så varliga genom lunden med henne

Min fader skall jag giva min gån-gare grå
Allt under den linden så gröna
Som han skall rida till kyrkan uppå
I riden så varliga genom lunden med henne

Min syster skall jag giva mina guld-ringar sju
Allt under den linden så gröna
Som jag ej haft sen jag stod brud
I riden så varliga genom lunden med henne

Min broder skall jag giva mina hand-skar små
Allt under den linden så gröna
Som han skall ha lik-vart han går
I riden så varliga genom lunden med henne

Den ene så för dom till Frejas dop
Allt under den linden så gröna
Den andre så för dom till Vallhalla sal
I riden så varliga genom lunden med henne

O, Silibrand went up to the high loft
All under the green linden tree
There he saw his daughter going to the grove
Ye ride so gracefully through the grove with her

O, woe is me, woe is me, what do I see
All under the green linden tree
I see my daughter coming to me
Ye ride so gracefully through the grove with her

O, Silibrand spread out his cloak so blue
All under the green linden tree
And upon it she did bear two baby boys
Ye ride so gracefully through the grove with her

I shall give my father my gray horse
All under the green linden tree
So he can ride to the church upon it
Ye ride so gracefully through the grove with her

I shall give my sister my seven golden rings
All under the green linden tree
That I haven't worn since I was a bride
Ye ride so gracefully through the grove with her

I shall give my brother my small hand gloves
All under the green linden tree
That he shall take with him wherever he goeth
Ye ride so gracefully through the grove with her

One child they took to Freya's baptism
All under the green linden tree
The other they took to the hall of Valhalla
Ye ride so gracefully through the grove with her

I Riden Så

Ye Ride So Gracefully

Trad. Swedish
Arr. Kimy Pedersen

I Riden Så is an old Swedish song about a man named Silibrand who sees his daughter under a linden tree, and lays out his cloak for her to lie on as she gives birth to twins. Unfortunately, both babies do not survive. It is possible that this song pre-dates Sweden's conversion to Christianity, as it features several pagan symbols such as the Norse goddess Freya, and the hall of Valhalla (an ancient custom is that when people die in combat, half are taken by the goddess Freya and the other half go to Valhalla.) The gray horse is another symbol of death, as Silibrand and his daughter ride the horse to take one baby to Freya, and the other to Valhalla.

Other interpretations suggest that Silibrand is already dead, and is watching over his daughter, that the twins grow up to be warriors and die in combat (hence one going to Freya and the other Valhalla), or that the daughter dies after giving birth, explaining why she gives her possessions to family members.

LYRICS

Bittida en morgon innan solen upprann
Innan foglarna började sjunga
Bergatrollet friade till fager ungersven
Hon hade en falskeliger tunga

-Herr Mannelig herr Mannelig trolofven i mig-
-För det jag bjuder så gerna-
-I kunnen väl svara endast ja eller nej-
-Om i viljen eller ej-

Eder vill jag gifva de gångare tolf
Som gå uti rosendelunde
Aldrig har det varit någon sadel uppå dem
Ej heller betsel uti munnen

Eder vill jag gifva de qvarnarna tolf
Som stå mellan Tillö och Ternö
Stenarna de äro af rödaste gull
Och hjulen silfverbeslagna

Eder vill jag gifva ett förgyllande svärd
Som klingar utaf femton guldringar
Och strida huru I strida vill
Stridsplatsen skolen i väl vinna

Eder vill jag gifva en skjorta så ny
Den bästa I lysten att slita
Inte är hon sömnad av nål eller trå
Men virkat av silket det hvita

Sådana gåfvor jag toge väl emot
Om du vore en kristelig qvinna
Men nu så är du det värsta bergatroll
Af Neckens och djävulens stämma

Bergatrollet ut på dörren sprang
Hon rister och jämrar sig svåra
Hade jag fått den fager ungersven
Så hade jag mistat min plåga

Early one morning before the sun rose
Before the birds began to sing
The mountain troll proposed to the handsome young man
She had a false tongue

-Sir Mannelig, Sir Mannelig, won't you marry me-
-For what I offer so generously?-
-You can answer only yes or no-
-Will you, or not?-

I would give you twelve great horses
That graze in rose groves
They have never worn a saddle
Nor had a bit in their mouths

I would give you twelve fine mills
That stand between Tillo and Terno
The mill stones are made of the reddest gold
And the wheels are silver-plated

I would give you a gilded sword
That jingles from fifteen gold rings
And fight with it in battle as you would like
On the battlefield you will win

I would give you a brand new shirt
The best and most lustrous to wear
It is not sewn with a needle or thread
But crocheted with white silk

"Gifts such as these I would receive well
If you were a Christian woman
But I know you are the worst mountain troll
From the offspring of water spirits and the devil"

The mountain troll ran out the door
She shaked and wailed so loudly
"Had I gotten that handsome young man
I would have been freed from my torment"

Herr Mannelig

Sir Mannelig

Trad. Swedish
Arr. Kimy Pedersen

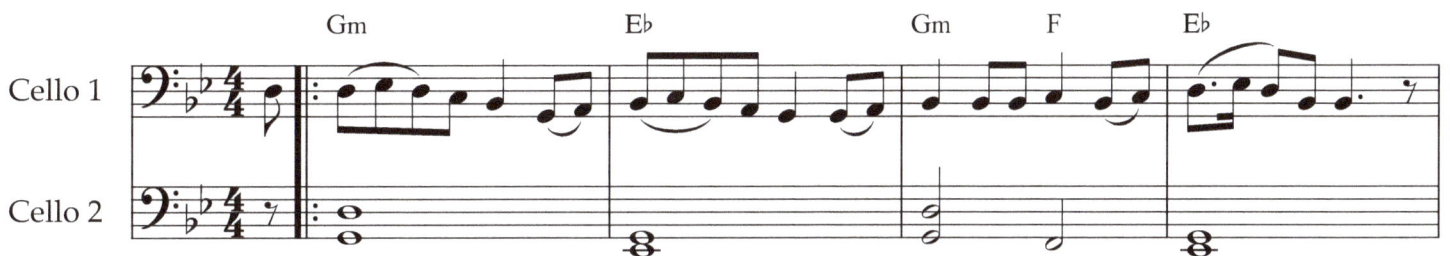

Herr Mannelig is a Swedish ballad about a mountain troll who proposes to a young human man (Sir Mannelig), probably trying to deceive him. She tries to bribe him with several gifts, but he ultimately refuses temptation because she is a troll and not a human Christian woman (this ballad was presumably written after Christianity became the dominant religion in Sweden). This song was first transcribed in the late 1800s, but it is unknown when the ballad was written.

Schottis efter Luringen och Spel-Bengten #1

Schottis from Luringen and Spel-Bengten #1

Trad. Swedish schottis
Arr. Kimy Pedersen

This schottishe (called "schottis" in Swedish) comes from the repertoire of Luringen and Spel-Bengten. They were two fiddle players in the 19th centrury from southern Sweden and were known for playing unconventional folk tunes, many of which accompany dances. A schottische is a partnered dance and several European countries have variations of them.

Nuku Nuku Nurmilintu
Sleep, Sleep, Grassland Bird

Trad. Finnish lullaby
Arr. Kimy Pedersen

LYRICS

Nuku, nuku nurmilintu,
Väsy, väsy, västäräkki.
Nuku nurmelle hyvälle,
Vaivu maalle valkialle.

Lintu tuopi liinahapaijan,
Haapana hyvän hamehen.
Kaskeloinen korvatyynyn,
Pääskynen peäalusen.

Sleep, sleep, little grassland bird,
Tired, tired, white wagtail.
Sleep in the grass,
Drift into the white land.

The birds will bring you a linen shirt,
A wigeon will bring you a nice skirt.
A koskelo will bring you a little pillow,
The swallows will make you a cushion.

This song is an old Finnish lullaby. The grassland bird represents a child that is being sung to sleep. It is possible that this song is about a mother mourning the loss of her child, as the narrator urges the bird to "sleep in the grass" and "drift into the white land," which could represent the bird/child transitioning to an afterlife.

Himlens Polska

Trad. Finnish polska
Arr. Kimy Pedersen

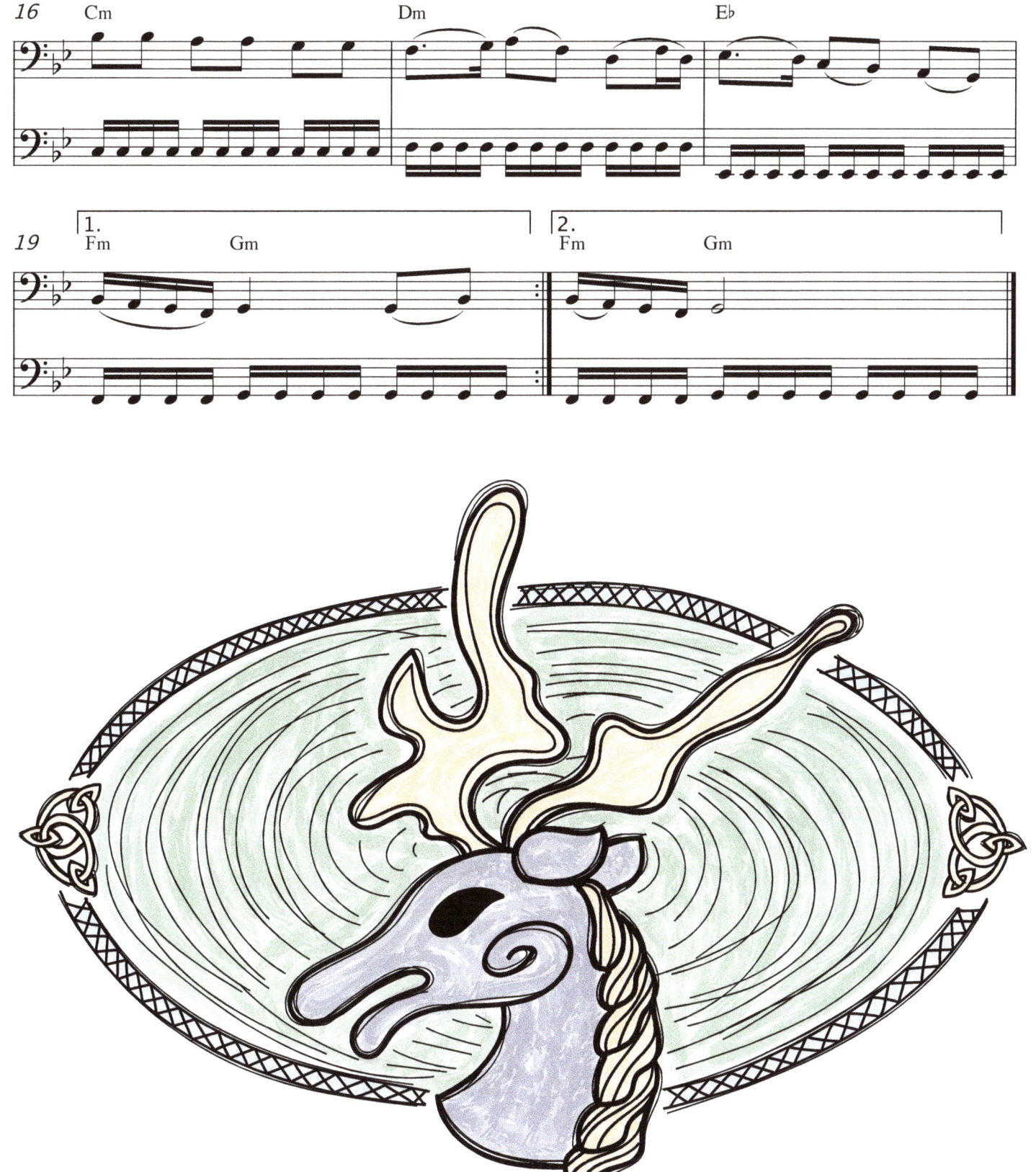

LYRICS

Kalliolle, kukkulalle
rakennan minä majani (x2)
Tule, tule, tyttö nuori,
jakamaan se mun kanssani! (x2)

Jos et sinä mulle tule,
lähden täältä kauas pois (x2)
muille maille vierahille,
jost' en koskaan palaa pois (x2)

Kyllähän sen varmaan tiedän,
etten minä sua saa (x2)
Tyydyn onneeni, olen yksin,
aina muistan sinua (x2)

Eipä tässä asiassa
auta arvo, rikkaus (x2)
Siinä koettaa voimiansa
kahden nuoren rakkaus (x2)

Jos oon mieltäsi pahottanna
jollakulla tavalla (x2)
Pyydän anteeksi tällä kertaa.
tapojain en paranna! (x2)

On the rocky hill,
is where I will build my house.
Come, come, young lady,
so you can share it with me!

If you don't come with me,
I will leave and go far away.
To other countries to find guests
and I will never return.

Yes, I know for sure
that it will not happen.
I will live alone,
and I will always remember you.

In this case,
value and wealth will not help.
It will test the strength
of the love of two young people.

If my words have hurt you
in some way.
I'll apologize this time,
but I won't heal!

Kalliolle Kukkulalle
On the Rocky Hill

Trad. Finnish
Arr. Kimy Pedersen

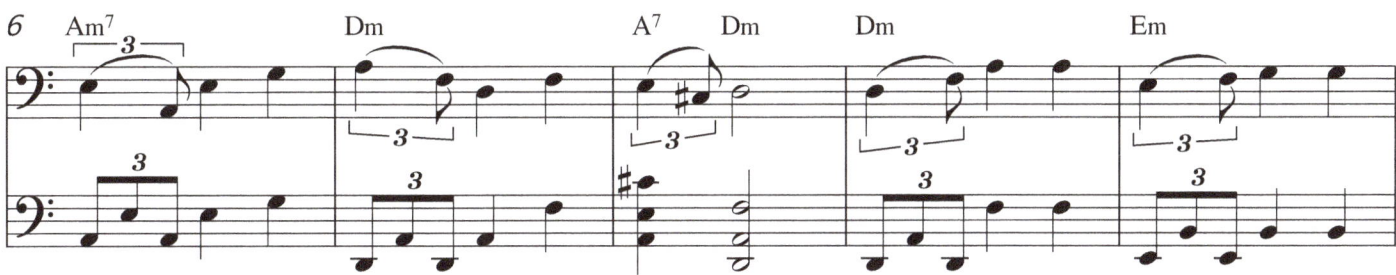

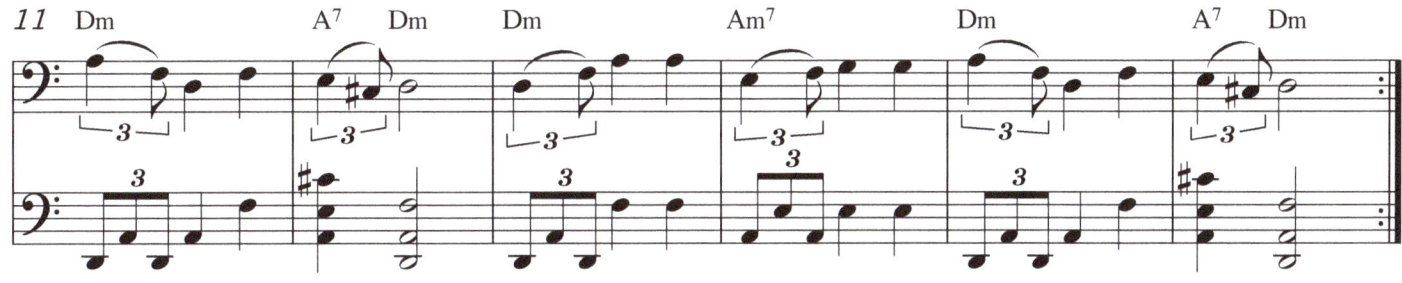

Kalliolle Kukkulalle tells the story of someone who wants to build a house, and a life, with the person they are in love with. It is unclear if the love is unrequited or not, but the narrator warns the love interest that if she refuses to live with them, they will go to foreign lands to find a new lover and never be seen again.

Jos Mun Tuttuni Tulisi
If the One I Knew Came Now

Trad. Finnish
Arr. Kimy Pedersen

LYRICS

Jos mun tuttuni tulisi,
Ennen nähtyni näkyisi;
Sillen suuta suikkajaisin,
Jos olis suu suden veressä;
Sillen kättä käppäjäisin,
Jospa kärme kämmenpäässä!

Olisko tuuli mielellissä,
Ahavainen kielellissä!
Sanan toisi, sanan veisi,
Kahden rakkaan välillä!

Enemmbä heitän herku-ruat,
Paistit pappilan unohdan;
Kuin mä heitän hertaiseni,
Kesän kestyteldyäni,
Talven taivutelduani.

If the one I knew came now,
if my love should appear,
I would kiss him on the mouth,
even if it were tainted with wolf's blood;
I would grab and hold his hand,
even if a serpent were between his fingers.

If the wind had a conscience,
If it had a language,
to speak and return the words
that two lovers say.

I would disregard any luxury,
Even the savory meat at a priest's house,
rather than forsake the friend of my heart,
who I hunted in the summer,
and tamed in the winter.

Jos Mun Tuttuni Tulisi is a old Finnish love song and poem that describes the yearning and desire that someone can feel for someone they love. It is thought that this song is sung from a woman's point of view, but other interpretations suggest the narrator could be of any gender. This song was first transcribed and published in 1840 by Elias Lönnrot. There are several versions of this song, and it is often considered to be a version of a closely related song, Kun Mun Kultani Tulisi.

Sofa Urtubörn
Seal Babies Sleep

Trad. Icelandic lullaby
Arr. Kimy Pedersen

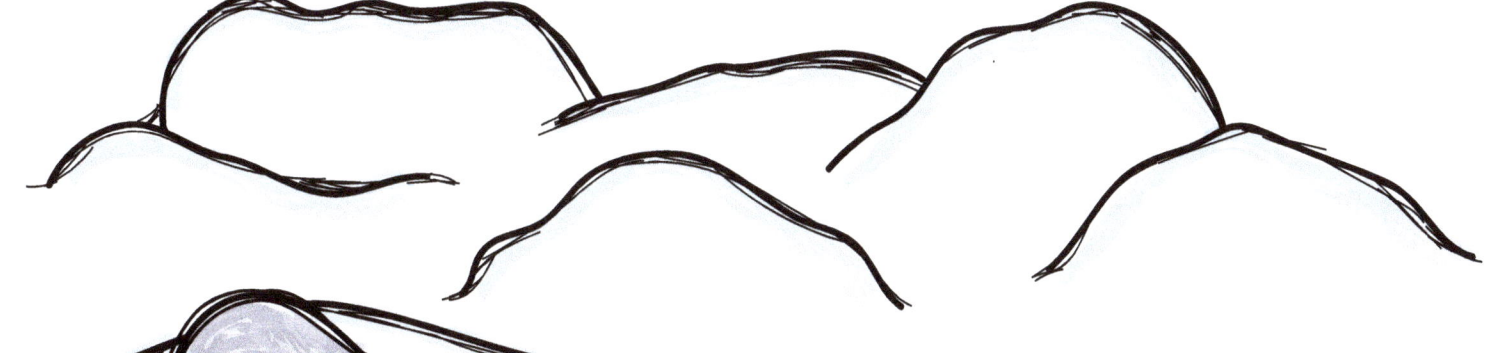

LYRICS

Sofa Urtubörn
á útskejum, veltur sjór yfir
og enginn þau svæfir

Sofa kisubörn
á kerhlemmum, murra og mala
og enginn þau svæfir

Sofa grýlubörn
á grjóthólum, urra og ýla
og enginn þau svæfir

Sofa bolabörn
á báshellum, moð fyrir múla
og enginn þau svæfir

Sofa mannabörn
í mjúku rúmi, bía og kveða
og pabbi þau svæfir

Seal babies sleep
on a rock far from the coast,
the sea rolls over
and no one lulls them to sleep

Kittens sleep
on the lid of a pot, they grumble
and purr
lulls them to sleep

The children of the Grýla sleeps
in a rocky cave, they growl and howl
and no one lulls them to sleep

Calves sleep
on the stall's slab, hay leavings for
the mules
and no one lulls them to sleep

A man's babies sleep
in a soft bed, lulling and chanting
and their father lulls them to sleep

Sofa Urtubörn is an Icelandic lullaby that describes babies of different species going to sleep. The Grýla is a giantess who eats naughty children. She is featured in Icelandic folklore, and is associated with Christmas. Her children are the Yule Lads,

thirteen boys who visit town one-by-one for each of the thirteen nights before Christmas to place small gifts in good childrens' shoes and place potatoes in shoes of naughty children.

Ó, Mín Flaskan Fríða
Oh, my beautiful flask!

Trad. Icelandic
Arr. Kimy Pedersen

LYRICS

Ó, mín flaskan fríða!
Flest ég vildi líða,
frostið fár og kvíða
fyrr en þig að missa.
Mundi' ég mega kyssa
munninn þinn, þinn, þinn?
Munninn þinn svo mjúkan finn,
meir en verð ég hissa.

Oh my beautiful flask!
I want to endure almost everything
a cold blizzard and anxiety,
instead of losing you.
I would kiss
your mouth, yours, yours?
Your mouth feels so soft and fine
I'm more than surprised.

This Icelandic drinking song romanticizes the flask that a person drinks from. There are originally three verses to this song, but the first verse is the only appropriate one for this book :)

The Hungry Innocent / Magáll Hvarf úr Eldhúsi

The Magáll Disappeared from the Kitchen

Trad. Icelandic
Arr. Kimy Pedersen

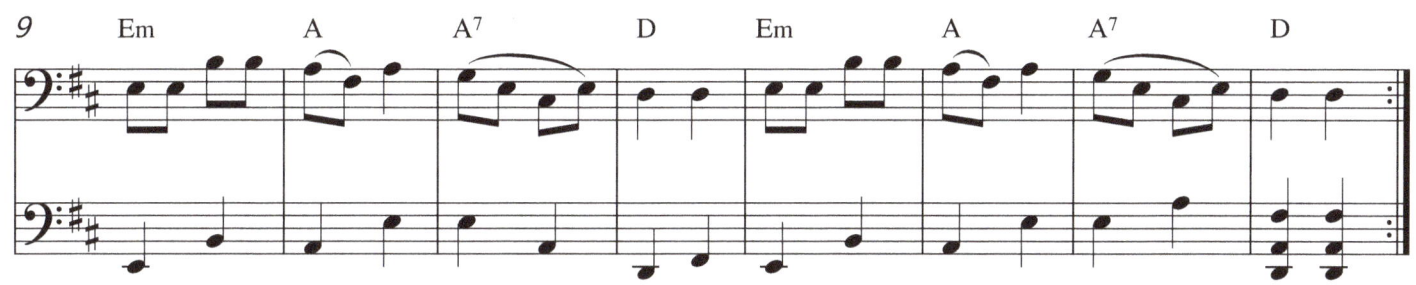

Magáll is a traditional Icelandic dish made of a smoked or fermented lamb flank. It is usually sliced and served on bread and is sometimes served today with pancakes and syrup. The process of making magáll is thought to have existed since the Middle Ages.

(information from the Slow Food Foundation for Biodiversity)

LYRICS

Ólafur reið með björgum fram,
villir hann, stillir hann
hitti'hann fyrir sér álfarann, þar rauður logi brann.
Blíðan lagði byrinn undan björgunum,
blíðan lagði byrinn undan björgunum fram.

Þar kom út ein álfamær,
villir hann, stillir hann
sú var ekki kristni kær, þar rauður logi brann.
Blíðan lagði byrinn undan björgunum,
blíðan lagði byrinn undan björgunum fram.

"Velkominn Ólafur Liljurós!
villir hann, stillir hann
Gakk í björg og bú með oss", þar rauður logi brann.
Blíðan lagði byrinn undan björgunum,
blíðan lagði byrinn undan björgunum fram.

"Ekki vil ég með álfum búa,
villir hann, stillir hann
heldur vil ég á Krist minn trúa", þar rauður logi brann.
Blíðan lagði byrinn undan björgunum,
blíðan lagði byrinn undan björgunum fram.

Hún gekk sig til arkar,
villir hann, stillir hann
tók upp saxið snarpa, þar rauður logi brann.
Blíðan lagði byrinn undan björgunum,
blíðan lagði byrinn undan björgunum fram.

Saxinu hún stakk í síðu,
villir hann, stillir hann
Ólafi nokkuð svíður, þar rauður logi brann.
Blíðan lagði byrinn undan björgunum,
blíðan lagði byrinn undan björgunum fram.

Ólafur leit sitt hjartablóð
villir hann, stillir hann
líða niður við hestsins hóf, þar rauður logi brann.
Blíðan lagði byrinn undan björgunum,
blíðan lagði byrinn undan björgunum fram.

Ei leið nema stundir þrjár,
villir hann, stillir hann
Ólafur var sem bleikur nár, þar rauður logi brann.
Blíðan lagði byrinn undan björgunum,
blíðan lagði byrinn undan björgunum fram.

Vendi ég mínu kvæði í kross
villir hann, stillir hann
sankti María sé með oss, þar rauður logi brann.
Blíðan lagði byrinn undan björgunum,
blíðan lagði byrinn undan björgunum fram

Olaf rode along the cliffs,
He's led astray, he is calm,
He comes across an elf-dwelling, there a red flame burned.
Mild was the breeze below the rocks,
Mild was the breeze below the rocks ahead.

An elven maid came out,
He's led astray, he is calm,
She was not a Christian girl there a red flame burned.
Mild was the breeze below the rocks,
Mild was the breeze below the rocks ahead.

"Welcome, Olaf Lilyrose!"
He's led astray, he is calm,
"Come to the cliffs and live with us," There a red flame burned.
Mild was the breeze below the rocks,
Mild was the breeze below the rocks ahead.

"I do not want to live with elves,"
He's led astray, he is calm,
"I would rather believe in Christ." There a red flame burned.
Mild was the breeze below the rocks,
Mild was the breeze below the rocks ahead.

She went to her chest,
He's led astray, he is calm,
She took a sharp sword, there a red flame burned.
Mild was the breeze below the rocks,
Mild was the breeze below the rocks ahead.

She stabbed the sword into his side,
He's led astray, he is calm,
Olaf is hurt, there a red flame burned.
Mild was the breeze below the rocks,
Mild was the breeze below the rocks ahead.

Olaf saw blood flowing from his heart,
He's led astray, he is calm,
He fell down to his horse's hoof, there a red flame burned.
Mild was the breeze below the rocks,
Mild was the breeze below the rocks ahead.

He suffered for three hours,
He's led astray, he is calm,
Olaf was a pink corpse, there a red flame burned.
Mild was the breeze below the rocks,
Mild was the breeze below the rocks ahead.

I give my song to the cross,
He's led astray, he is calm,
Saint Mary be with us, there a red flame burned.
Mild was the breeze below the rocks,
Mild was the breeze below the rocks ahead.

Ólafur Líljurós
Olaf and the Elf Maiden

Trad. Icelandic
Arr. Kimy Pedersen

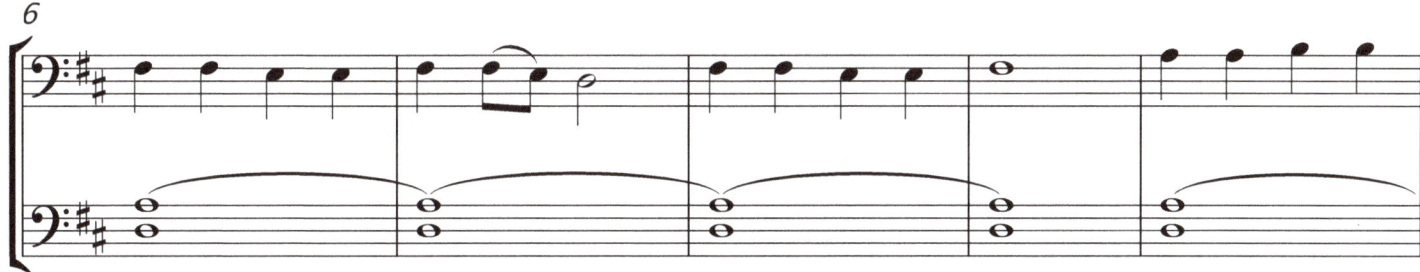

Ólafur Líljurós is an Icelandic ballad that tells the story of a young man who comes upon an "elven-dwelling." He meets an elven woman who tries to seduce him into living with the elves, but he refuses because he wants to remain Christian. The elven woman then draws a sword and kills him. It is probable that this song was written after Christianity was adopted by Iceland, and this song could possibly have an anti-pagan motive, as non-Christians (the elves) are the antagonists, and Ólafur refuses to give up his religion, which is seen in the song as admirable. Different versions of this song have been sung all over Scandinavia, including the Danish "Elveskud", Norwegian "Olaf liljekrans", Swedish "Herr Olof och Älvorna", and the Faroese "Ólavur riddarrós og álvarmoy".

Pindsvine Reinlander
Hedgehog Reinlander

Trad. Norwegian/
Danish reinlander
Arr. Kimy Pedersen

www.ingramcontent.com/pod-product-compliance
Lightning Source LLC
Chambersburg PA
CBHW040752020526
44118CB00042B/2906